Come, Take a Gentle Stab

THE ARAB LIST

SALIM BARAKAT

Come, Take a Gentle Stab

SELECTED POEMS

TRANSLATED BY
HUDA FAKHREDDINE AND JAYSON IWEN

LONDON NEW YORK CALCUTTA

SERIES EDITOR
Hosam Aboul-Ela

Seagull Books, 2023

© Salim Barakat, 2021

First published in English translation by Seagull Books, 2021
English translation © Huda Fakhreddine and Jayson Iwen, 2021

ISBN 978 1 8030 9 195 2

British Library Cataloguing-in-Publication Data
A catalogue record for this book is available from the British Library

Typeset by Seagull Books, Calcutta, India
Printed and bound by WordsWorth India, New Delhi, India

CONTENTS

ACKNOWLEDGEMENTS

Excerpts from 'Dylana and Diram' have appeared in a special online feature in *World Literature Today*: https://bit.ly/32moQkf (last accessed on 17 April 2021).

'Fog Composed Like a Gentleman' has appeared in *Nimrod* 62(2) (2019): 76–9.

Excerpts from *Syria* have appeared in *Arablit Quarterly* 2 (2019): 6–9.

An earlier version of 'Digression in an Abridged Context' has appeared in *Middle Eastern Literatures* 22(1) (2019): 134–53.

Portions of the Foreword have been excerpted from Huda Fakhreddine, 'Salīm Barakāt's Poetry as Linguistic Conquest: . . . the shot that kills you, may you recover', *Middle Eastern Literatures* 22(1) (2019): 134–53.

Salim Barakat is a Kurdish-Syrian poet and novelist, born in 1951 in
Qamishli, an ethnically, religiously and linguistically diverse city in
northern Syria. He moved to Damascus in the early 1970s and then
went on to Beirut. In 1982, the escalating political and sectarian ten-
sions in that war-torn city forced him to leave for Cyprus, where he
remained for over 15 years. He has resided in Sweden since 1999.
Barakat is often listed among the most prominent writers in Arabic.
He is, in addition, the most distinctive among those included under
the umbrella of writers of the 'Arabic prose poem', a term loosely
equivalent to 'free verse' in English. His language is intimidatingly
dense and complex, displaying a vast and daunting vocabulary. His
texts are the products of an aggressive and intimate excavation of the
Arabic language's creative and logical potential. He achieves the
'poetic', both in his poetry and prose, through a deliberate occlusion
of meaning behind a textured and thickened language. If meaning is
vision, an organizing of language into a coherent finality, Barakat's
poetry is a resistance to precisely that. 'Poetry,' he states, is a 'bloody
wager that drains language, like blood-letting, so it may either live
or die.'[1] It is a violent and deliberate dispelling of the comfort and
familiarity we impose upon words.

---

1 Salim Barakat, *al-Taʿjīl fī qurūḍ al-nathr* (Expediting the Loans of Prose)
(Damascus: Dār Zamān, 2010), pp. 166–7.

Throughout his career, Barakat has acquired the reputation for being not only a 'difficult' poet but also a 'difficult' man.[2] He is a very private person who rarely appears in the media, whether intentionally or unintentionally. His isolation and reluctance to engage with literary circles pre-date his move to Sweden. Even while in Beirut, friends and acquaintances tell stories about his idiosyncratic and often unruly behaviour. Mahmoud Darwish remembers the following incident in *A Memory for Forgetfulness*:

> He has taken the cultural life of Beirut by storm, overnight. He defends his writing ferociously, with his fists, because he doesn't believe in dialogue among intellectuals, considering it a mere babble. Taking his pistol and his showy muscles, he goes into the appropriate coffee shop and lies in wait for lesser critics who write for the cultural pages of daily papers, and doesn't mince his words about what they'd written against him. One time I said to him, 'Vladimir Mayakovsky used to treat his critics the same way in Gorky Street.' 'This is the only true criticism of criticism,' he answered.[3]

Referring to Barakat by only his first initial, S., Darwish points to characteristics which apply to both his conduct and his writing. He is 'the neighborhood's eloquent rooster [. . .] Lover of pistols, language, and exposed flesh [. . .] S. the Kurd [. . .] is elated by the war: it has allowed his repressed violence to emerge and ally itself with chaos.'[4] Needless to say, Barakat does not subscribe to the image of the poet

---

2 Barakat, *al-Taʿjīl*, p. 115.

3 Mahmoud Darwish, *Memory for Forgetfulness* (Ibrahim Muhawi trans.) (Los Angeles: University of California Press, 2013), pp. 78–9.

4 Darwish, *Memory for Forgetfulness*, p. 83.

as a cultured and refined person. More interestingly, as portrayed in the incident Darwish narrates above, Barakat deliberately and defiantly performs the stereotype of the Kurd in Arab societies as the disruptive and thuggish other.

Barakat's provocative persona and his confrontational relationship with Arabic are often tied to his preoccupation with what critics have called 'Kurdish themes'. Barakat insists on presenting himself as a Kurd who writes in Arabic. He is blunt in describing his relationship with the Arabic language to which he is both insider and outsider. Arabic is not his first language, but he defiantly plunders it and lays claim to it. Other poets and writers have validated this claim. In the blurbs on the back of the second volume of his collected works, *al-Dīwān*, which came out in 2017, the following endorsements by a host of Arab poets and writers appear: 'Since he invaded the Arabic poetic scene, Salim Barakat has heralded a different kind of poetry' (Darwish); '*Mawlānā*! What have you left for us? Release Arabic poetry from your grip' (Nizar Qabbani); 'the greatest Kurd since Salah al-Din/ Saladin' (Sa'di Yusuf). It is Adonis, however, who puts it most succinctly: 'The Arabic language is in this Kurdish poet's pocket.'[5] These endorsements reflect the bold and transgressive ethos of Barakat's work. In *al-Ta'jīl*, collected meditations on poetry and writing, he consistently refers to the Arabs in the third person, deliberately excluding himself from them: 'My Arabic language enlists the Arab as a partner in my Kurdishness, a partnership in the heritage of imagination.'[6] With his work, Arabic readers are on the threshold of comprehension,

---

5 Salim Barakat, *Al-Dīwān 2* (Damascus: Dār al-Madā, 2017). Most of these blurbs are excerpted from a special issue of the journal *Hajalnama* featuring Salim Barakat: *Hajalnama* 11–12 (2007): 181–223. *Hajalnama* is a Kurdish cultural journal published in Sweden.

6 Barakat, *al-Ta'jīl*, p. 102.

exceedingly conscious of themselves as explorers of what has thus far eluded them.

Barakat's work has been translated into Swedish, Spanish, Catalan, French, Kurdish and Turkish. A volume of selected poems titled *Syrie et autres poèmes* translated into French by Antoine Jockey recently won the Max Jacob Poetry Prize. Aside from a few excerpts translated in journals and studies, this is the first book-length translation of his work into English. Our selections span his entire career thus far, from the very first poem he published in the Damascene weekly magazine *al-Tali'a* in 1971 to his 2019 collection *The Lineages of Animal*. Our selections reflect his developing craft and his ongoing interrogation of poetic language and form. Our process usually begins with a literal translation that we then work on together, back and forth, to turn it into a poetic text in English. The conversation itself, our misreadings, misunderstandings and our efforts to resolve them often reveal dimensions of the text that initially eluded us both.

Our selections include excerpts from long poems such as 'Dylana and Diram' and book-length poems such as *Syria* and *All the Doors*. In them, Barakat builds a structure from the seemingly chaotic, presenting his reader with a daunting text that requires persistence, patience and, most of all, a surrender to exultation in language. We were careful while excerpting from these texts to maintain the tension and overall arc of emotion and rhythm which holds the pieces together.

Barakat's posture towards language involves processes of uncovering, reclaiming and de-familiarizing. He does not deny that it is also a difficult posture, one that does not come easy either to him or to his reader. He is nevertheless unfalteringly committed to it, although at times he does not hide his bitterness and frustration at the lack of acknowledgement by others, what he calls the 'unjust silence' (*al-ṣamt al-lā munṣif*)[7] with which his work has been received thus far:

> I don't know why I should go up the wooden stairs to the attic in one country and descend the wooden stairs into the cave of writing in another, seven days a week, in summer, winter, autumn and spring, at the same hour, and submit myself to a perilous terrifying test of the blank page and its claws [. . .]. But I know I have readers whose abilities texts cannot take lightly. They are demanding and just.[8]

His consolation is an imagined reader, someone who is willing to follow the signs and reach beyond the easy binaries—a reader as demanding as the text Barakat performs for us.

---

7 Barakat, *al-Taʿjīl*, p. 118.

8 Barakat, *al-Taʿjīl*, p. 118.

*Those Who Enter
and Those Who Exit,
All Shall Hail Me*

(1973)

Come, Dinoka Breva, Take a Gentle Stab!

(Excerpt)

When the packs of wolves descend from the north, dragging their asses through the snow, howling and setting the locked barns and throats of dogs ablaze, I hear Dinoka's death rattle.

In the watermelon fields around the villages, the sky used to scatter, revealing a void canopied by cobwebs and policemen's caps. Dinoka emerges naked, leading a pack of jackals in a direction empty of shrapnel.

Dinoka!

What shall I say to the hunters who saddle their hounds on the slopes of Sinjar and the mountains of Abdelaziz? You are hiding somewhere, perhaps in a barn, breathing in the earth and the mangers. You are grand and damp and haunted by the harvest and me.

I hear your father calling: 'Dinoka . . .' I hear your mother calling: 'Dinoka, take this barley bread to the immigrants. Tell them to rest awhile.'

There were more and more of them, day after day . . . from Tashkent, Khuzestan, Armenia and southwest Russia. They carried their sails and bundles of fern to the peninsula, without shoes or scythes. You were too young to realize how much they needed water; how much they needed a madwoman or a widow to bury deep in the cracks of wilderness, so she could sprout lentils and grasshoppers in the years of exodus. You didn't know how the trench between Amuda and Mosissana brims with the carcasses of mules and amputated limbs. You didn't know from where the Bedouins get French rifles, and why they swell at the edges of the village before attacking with cloaks wrapped around their heads.

It is said: You sprang forth from the direction of wilderness, and Breva sprang from there too. From the direction of wilderness, God sprang forth and from there too sprang wonder and the bullet casings children dug from the palace trash. It is said you returned with a flock of merry ewes and a single ram that heaved like a warrior over every spot wet with piss.

Dinoka . . . Dinoka . . .

I am tired. I don't hear your voice when I behold the hillsides of M'airika and the hay-heavy carts of the Kurds.

A Decree: The Hunt

Daughter of my whoring days.
Your mule no longer hides you, nor does the wilderness or the wires.
And your ghost, this cleft one, I will prop up when it falters, to
prolong my chase.
Let your bird alight on a slope, beyond the funeral of my branches.
I am tied to the orbiting sphere, to the whispers and the shadow of
the guillotine.

* * *

Beyond the trees,
on their loom, weavers have spun the threads of truce between
despair and the world. Beyond the trees, my lungs slumbered,
leaning against dry trunks, and were set ablaze.

I set the poor weavers on fire. They shook me and fell clinging to my
flowers and plants. They took refuge in the gloves of a woman who
retreats from Bedouins trembling before my gaping veins.

Beyond the trees are water lamps and dust. Through it, I witness
your hands melting . . .
Kneel down, daughter of my whoring days!
Neither the wilderness nor the wires can hide you now. Beside a
thicket or a mountain, you and I will watch my rain fall and my day
bend, tossed back and forth by benevolence, by winds and the
shadow of the guillotine.

You shall see the birds of my oblivious blood

(I have vowed to ignore them, as becomes noblemen,

never to acknowledge them before the guards and slave girls of the

Republic).

You shall see my blood

swamped with sea kings and city brick.

I ignore people who come and go. I pierce the soles of my shoes so I

may know what a tramp knows of martyrs, abandoned on paths to

the mausoleum,

so I may know how my time appeases me,

how the prairies swarm with grass that saddens me

(I am saddened by lightning when it strikes the edges of the flood;

saddened by the flood when it swells ashore; saddened by the shore

when banished from history by the state; saddened when sorrow

deserts the state; saddened by sorrow.)

Standing behind you, Daughter of my whoring days,

I summon the jujube leaves to a people's bewilderment: 'Hurry to

my suburb, O Jujube of Syria! Hurry, by God! For I am mesmerized

by a smoke that holds me from the freedom of generations hunting

generations. My horizon is saddles and battle dust, and by it I sug-

gest another name for my water. I accompany the mammals of this

age to the great hall of salamander and hyacinth. I lead them to a

breast that God has taken by surprise behind the wheat stalk.

O Jujube, the geographers are asleep and the bullets have been

loaded with the secrets of grass.

'I am the skipper and my ship is the rusty trail.' You see my blood all

about you, circling an abyss within my abyss, frightening a herd of desolation's mares stretching within the fences of the soul, neighing beneath Breva's gown as strangers and the rites of the gods slay her. I choose vehemence and tie the entrails of the mares to a post against which the Circassians and the Kurds rub themselves and stand erect.

With Narcissus and unwavering faith, I seal their buds, and like trees and birds we head for the river,
'Come along, O river!
'Come along, O mountain!' we say.
'Come along, O partridge!
'And you, O leaves of jujube, come to the desert that spills from a crack in the skull!'

[. . .]

A.
There is no space in my atoms but the rustling of the bright rain's pants.
—Break down.
—I break down.
Let my death-rattle break down the squares, so I might rejoice in flags besieging the Revolution, resisting those who come together.

B.

There is no space in my atoms but the people's indulgence.
—Break down.
—I break down,
and I threaten those who come to me unified.

C.

There is no space in my atoms but the germs of war.
Come to me,
paramours, crypts and desolate moons dangling from hunger and
telephone poles. Come to me melted in the tin of commotion so I
may reshape you and hand each team its orbit of grenade. I am an
inheritor of your women, for I take the mother on the daughter's bed,
unite the two sisters under the blade of my breath,
and lead your rituals at the port of roses, which ship off goddesses
and the days of glory,
a boat overcrowded with alembics of blasphemy.

D.

There is no space in my atoms but the roots of Khursan.
—Break down.
—I will not break down in a detention camp
I can escape from to the plague. Come to me, schemers and sodomites.
Come, all you addicts and let us take my alarms by surprise.

I listened to the world
I listened to Dinoka Breva

I listened to my impression and my drowsiness,
I listened to a love that lulls me in the stupor of sedition, establishes
a peace timed by the eyelashes of women growing denser, women
overflowing the chimneys of the poor.

[...]

Untranslatable gazelles and yet I translate them:
'Each gazelle is a beginning.'
And on the hills, I translate the banners: 'We awoke to find you a
splinter conveying the sand family to the helmet, and the Arab to a
memory within the sodium of the Universe.
We called you by your name.
We called you in the name of the diamond and the pearl; helpless
you were
and like muscles your destinations slackened, and you sagged,
and ants collected what fell from you to the earth,
cell
by cell
by cell.
You rose up into a creature built of stones before Christ and after.
We saw you cry out: 'I am the Brahman of ants! I drive them into my
kingdom of lamentation where we killed you.'
Bless my throat
under the retreat of clouds, banner by banner, I hustle my day
towards Dinoka's wheat stalks:

'What does someone like me do but corner someone like you for the slaughter. What else but examine your organs after the slaughter and go mad, demanding the death of man and the death of sea and the death of all metals and oxides the future might fashion to create its foetuses?
What can I do beyond trees?

[. . .]

Whom do I call upon in the seclusions of geography, whom do I call upon to witness my massacre asking for water from pools at the intersection of the world and God?

[. . .]

I said: Tomorrow I will set out towards a tomorrow that retreats or turns
a corner before the limits of the human;
I heard the human wrap up his present and die. I rush to the wheat stalk so it may tell Dinoka I'm on my way.
I carry a few excuses scribbled down, lest I stutter when I see her, and always with me, I carry my abyss.

Union of Lineages

'This is my modern face.'

Here I come.

Let every little beggar king in the land of apostasy be wary of where
the stabbing will come from.

At the limits of desolation in the eyes of God's waitress and maidens,
I abridge the frightened time in the female eye.

I shove the Qurayshi time to it.

Neither tears nor the blood of the poor can stop this wandering,
my roving
after caravans of fluff . . . Let him beware.

Let every little beggar king in the land of apostasy be wary of where
the stabbing will come from.

'This is my modern face.'

Shoeless I travel towards Persia and the Byzantine capitals. I raise
my face to the darkness asking, and I ask my bloodied feet about the
blind land and the heavenly whispers of bats,
and standing in the palm of exile, I shall scream:

O people of Syria, the war steeds are whinnying at the gates of the
Kaaba and I alone

spread my cloak for those who seek refuge in the shadow of black stone.

I am torn apart when death dangles over the pilgrims' heads.

Between the bare chest and the thirsty spear, I coalesce.

I crowd the kingdom of terror into a crack, parting the cargo of the panting time

before and behind me.

I rise in the breath of the Kaaba, a smouldering the desert exhales as it drags the clamour of its tribes towards songs of war.

I fasten the lineages of he who goes on foot and he who mounts, he who flees and he who stands his ground in the fray, until the wailing palm tree drapes a wing of tears about me . . .

In the rattle of spears, I pledge allegiance to my banner

and I strike east, west. I strike in despair . . . and my first face falls.

I strike . . . and my second face falls

I retreat the pilgrims to Arafat as dust crumbling under the hooves of the shattering winds.

We then die, so we may dream.

We then rise, so we may dream.

We then open veins, so we may see in blood the coming of trees with the new day,

wrapping the joy of rivers like turbans about their tops.

Pike

(1980)

From **'Dylana and Diram'**

A mountain goat on a hill
and a stillness that raises its horns high as a mountain goat.
Don't move a step closer, O guide!
Don't move a step further.
Your place is the place from which roots eye roots
and the earth eyes its inheritance.

A mountain goat on a hill
and a stubborn stillness raising its horns high as the goat.

1.

Look at her, a heap of blond baskets under the flashing of your
blood, Diram. Look, how she sleeps upon your arm, her breaths
falling star after star in the vastness of your virility. . . . Do you
remember, Diram, the time you came to her, timid, wrapped in
fields, your steps the steps of day, and your clamour the clamour of
wheat stalks? Do you remember the evening that glittered in your
eyes, that first evening when you both plundered with kisses the
treasures of being, and uncovered a strange stream under the
bedrock of the soul? Easy, Diram! Let it be slow, your enchantment

of the chambers of her heart—Dylana's heart, which hangs like a beat, full of life.

2.

Look at him. A blond arrow under the flashing of your blood, Dylana. See how he decorates the evening with the rattle of his manhood. He climbs to you on a ladder of gasps, as if all luxury is his, as if you are the words by which he chants the song of man. Sing to him what the cloud sings to its daughter. Come down from your cloying sweetness and reveal the seduction of heights, so you may take the field of his heart with the wheat of your song? Come, Dylana, he is leaning closer, narrating fruit.

3.

Look at her, see how she graces your chest with a ray of lips and fingers. Look at her, Diram, and you shall see twenty hearts beneath her heart. Each heart hallucinates another twenty from its dream. She is the river's mouth to every man anointed with the rumble of roots. She is the seeping of hours and arguments, the final drain of every bravery or fear. Don't move a step closer, Diram! Don't move a step further! Your place is the place from which sweetness spies itself asleep in blond baskets and blood.

4.

Rise, Dylana, and tighten your soft siege. You are the forest where his line shall flourish and the entrails mix with birds. You are his rattling amid rattling. You are his praise, in which every king sees his kingdom and every tramp a path to the throne. So when he leans over you, raise to him the vessel of woman and to his trembling chest raise the shield of your bosom, bloodied with clouds and the ages.

5.

Rise, Diram! Stand up to see from the peaks of mirth the slope of woman spread from glaring masks to song. You are the sword to her springs. With you she strikes the mornings and they split open into longings and elk. You are her breath among breaths and her praise in which air dips the stray arrows of gods. So when she leans over you, raise to her mouth your mouth, studded with the song of man, and to her trembling bosom raise the shield of your bosom, stippled with water and eulogies.

6.

Look at him, Dylana! See how he gathers thunderbolts and scatters winds over your bed. See how he dangles from your gasping like fruit. He lays traps for plants as if bragging of you to the penetrance of water. See how he surrounds water like land, so he may besiege your heartbeat rising, like foam and ships, from water. . . . When he opens his net at close of day, scattering planets and pike-fish, let him sleep in his prophecies. Let him be, Dylana. All he grasps of the earth is a handful of brick, and all he sees is the slope of your breast spreading over earth a shadow of evening and manhood.

7.

Look at her, Diram! See how she gathers flocks of geese before your heart and weaves the clouds. See how she sways towards you, herd by herd from the farthest slope, hand in hand with the gathering horizon. When she leaps streams, her dress reveals roots that do not touch the earth but graze the praises with which all roots cover themselves. If you decide to take her hand in yours, you take the horizon too. If you decide to hold her, then let the roots hold you; may fruit sip fruit from your breath; may the earth rush to you, unsheathing her flood of milk and forms.

8.

Wake him, Dylana! Wake him from a sleep embroidered with the sweetness of a thousand drunken hearts. Wake the morning with him so they may set out together towards you, dusted with lust, with opulence, with glee. For he is the last one you'll see hallucinating, blowing into illusory horns, filling, like a servant, the cups of the drowned with heroism. There, he stands, in his own gale, in the ancient gusting of roots and the rejoicing of the wild in the wild. He is the last one you will see approaching like the sign a storm sends before it wears bloody armour and yanks away the tablecloth, shattering plates against the soul's marble. Wake him. Wake him up, Dylana.

9.

Wake her, Diram! Wake the butterfly of the unseen and its golden
dragonfly. . . . Wake Dylana and, with her, wake the house, stone by
stone, and then the square around the house and then the fence.
And when that's done, wake the morning which sleeps by the fence.
Say: Come, Dylana, come let us witness the hesitant shining of the
earth as it sheds iron and splendour to our human shield. Come, let
us bare our breasts to the fields, trembling with the sweetness of a
spearhead sunk deep where the sesame and saffron flow. As if,
together, we strive to be wounds beyond which are no wounds.
Come, wake her, Diram.

10.

Wake him, Dylana! Wake the boy, his naked chest restless under a
pouring ray. Wake him, wake the day and the loaves. Fill your pail—
that from which you water the unseen animals of morning—fill it
with cocoons of silk and berries that fall from praise. Weave with
silk and berries the sweetness draped over Diram. Wake him. Wake
him up, Dylana.

11.

Wake her, Diram! Wake the dream from under her lashes. Throw
a pebble of time into her, may she quiver like the face of a spring;
may she widen ring by ring, each a carriage carrying herbs and
pathways. Come, by God, the messenger of the valleys is picking

bouquets of fog for you both and spreading lavender childhood over the fence by the house. Wake her. Wake her up, Diram.

12.

Wake him, Dylana! Wake the face of the charade, that boy encircled by the scythes of gods. Wake him so you may witness the hasty morning dew and its humorous seductions. May you know that the dew neighs in the grass and has horns that declare good-natured heresy in good-natured soil.

13.

Wake her, Diram! Wake the celestial pomp of Dylana. Scatter over her beads of morning and arrogance. If she spreads out before you, waking, study her the way a plant studies a plant. Sit together in the shade of kisses and let songs of songs seduce you. Wake her, Diram. Wake her up!

14.

Wake him, Dylana! Wake the human ray, Diram, as he drunkenly descends from the splendour of man. Don't drape your hands or your gasping over him. Let him extend, clear and lucent; buds and bunches looming within him. You will then possess him and all that looms within him. You can choose to be the human home of plant and cloud and wings. Dylana, wake him up!

15.

Wake her, Diram! Wake the living blood and its sympathetic forms. Crown yourself for Dylana's waking with gentle drumming. It is the waking of a throne by whose power the fountains rise and the streams run. She is your bow. With her you launch—when you launch—your self in a final song. Wake her, Diram, wake her up!

16.

Wake him, Dylana! Wake opulence and its sympathetic forms. Witness the opening of his eyelashes release birds. He is a wakefulness only morning knows, grasping the sound of water. He is your bow. With him you shoot—when you shoot—your entirety in a final song. Wake him, Dylana, wake him up!

17.

Wake her, Diram! Wake Dylana, an ocean of foam. Spread your sails when she twists under the sweep of your morning blood. Charge her blood with naked clouds. Wake her, Diram, wake her up!

Wake him up,
Wake her up,
I did not wish to wake the earth that morning.
The earth did not wish to wake me either.

Everything passes when the signs are complete, and he who grasps onto moaning will depart with morning. Thus, they set out—Dylana and Diram—and I did not wish to wake the earth that morning and it did not wish to wake me.

[. . .]

They were heading back and the earth too was heading back from its daily harvest of a thousand wheat stalks, a thousand blazes, a thousand intrusions where the brave have abandoned their destinies under an invisible wave, a thousand cracked shields, a thousand thunderbolts wet with kisses; a thousand men shot Dylana and Diram with arrows of ash; they bowed to the silence that scatters waters in its wake and ravages flowers.

Thus, they set out: a boy and a woman.

And I am a guide who led two lovers to naught but sweet futility. I knew when the heart inherits the river's mouth, it reveals itself, like a secret the delirious sheds. But I took them with me nevertheless—swaddled in lightning bolts that bloom into bitter halos—I took them towards an uninherited splendour, and there I said: Spread your sails like a rising star with which land listens for the tapping of water on water's shield . . .

By God, by God, do not ask me, after all this, do not ask me to narrate the earth, direction by direction, and the sky, bolt by bolt. I am the perpetuation of the story, and if I speak, I speak my heart scattering in the storm like copper sand grouses. No! Do not ask me, after all this, to narrate death with death, and to tread upon this sweetness like the void of a mule's hoof. Look, as you sit there on a sunset fence, look and you will see twenty men covering Diram and Dylana with their cloaks. Then, a single line of blood trickles brazenly among pebbles and straw, and disappears at the edge of desolation.

With the Same Traps,
with the Foxes That Ride the Winds

(1982)

Fog Composed Like a Gentleman

1.

It's the will that strikes the earth with its mask, and you are the echo
of the blow. So heave then. Wave, sliding from leaf to leaf, from gasp
to gasp, and chew eternity with chainsaw teeth.

Don't say the storm wrapped in a fur coat is yours. Don't say
sweetness is your whip with which you herd the vegetable horses,
and that the day is a goose that wandered from your iron enclosure.
Instead, search for the memory of apple in the words of a branch
and release your hands like powdered gold.

Your gazelle is there, your crystal gazelle, under a crystal tree. Your
heart is here, shaking its horns to frighten the fur-clad dawn from
your bed, which drops to depths where not even slumber herds its
white cattle.

It's the will that strikes the earth with its mask, and you are the echo
of the blow.

2.

Let's negotiate like two gentlemen.
Sit in front of me. I will sit here. I have what you want.
Stare at me as befits an enemy, then empty your pockets on the
table. First, the garden. I see roots poking from your shirt. I see dirt
on your hands. Come, put it all on the table . . . the garden first.

And hand over the cloud that wets the rim of your hat. I see cold
strands hanging from your hair. Hand over the rainbow, the one
draped over your glistening vest. Hand it over . . . come . . . on the
table.

No. No. Don't be aloof. Let us talk like gentlemen. I have what you
want.

Sit in front of me. Put your magnificence, which has exhausted my
praise, on the table and the distance too; the distance of anger
framed like the portrait of a grandfather . . . hand it over. Hand over
the evening that hangs like a tie over your chest.

Open your jacket so I can see what's left in there. Yes, yes, a hidden
star, the remnants of a battle, nightingales asleep on a sword . . . place
them all here. All of it, including the burning that hasn't yet begun.

Don't be pale. I have what you want.

3.

Exhausted by gardens, bent like an arch extending from gold to praise,
this is how your shadow spans over my things.
Aided by your voice and your hearing, time walks the road
to the end of speech.
I confide in you the sparrow dead on a wire in the street,
I confide in you the mountain that can be seen from my window,
holding its hammer of fog over the ruins of dusk.
I confide in you the moaning of the door . . . I am he who sits here,
before the plate of the man who was murdered at the door. He
hasn't touched his food.

My prince, you, the vitality of darkness, you. Slip away from scandal
and come to me.

4.

'Fog composed as a gentleman treads upon the vegetable threshold,'
says the maid to her mistress. But you, standing with the arrogance
of one who has broken the flowerpots and disturbed the ivy,
standing before the garden with your shears and hoes, and on
your hands a faint trace of fertilizer.

You tread the same threshold the fog treads, seeing farther than the
maid sees, and you return shouting: 'Quiet! He's warning the plants.
With his carefree acrobatics, he conquers.'

Fog shoes
Fog crutches
Ancestors who have forgotten the entrance to your garden:
That's what you would never say yourself;
That's what the maid would never tell her mistress.

5.

Sesame ghosts raise the dawn like curtains.
O you delicious one, confused as the wing of a beetle. I open my
path to you like a wrestler with his spear and snare.
My breath is kicking and my sweat descends like storms of soft fur.

You may slip from me here or slip from me there, delicious, confused
one. I am the confusion that achieves certainty, the sovereign
shadow that retreats and spreads. It is as if my fist alone were the
assurance with which doubt fortifies itself and in which the fugitive
hides from his exposed destiny.

Where do you go, my descendant?
You, desirable, woven by darkness, where do you go, delicious one?
All things are besieged by me. The springs are my quiver of arrows
and the day is my dog.

6.

With its swords of ice and catapults, the earth opens its path
towards me.
With its nihilistic cicadas and its peoples whom I can smell like
bitter cooking, with bearers who carry their insides like mail,
the earth opens its path towards me.
And I, like bridges, intent in my folly to squander the stranger's
inheritance and his destinies.

7.

Who will arrive, O Earth, who will arrive?
Sacrificial animals of marble. A burnished sunset and a playfulness
smeared with moaning. Scaffolds that support the city and a dawn
like a jacket. Tomorrow. Tomorrow. Leave your dogs at the door.
Leave the sunset. Get off the anchor. For the depths are your depths.
Tomorrow. Tomorrow. Like an ascendant, no, like wisdom under
an ivy leaf, the frivolous dust watches you. And your tools? No. A
transparency supports the polished machine. Waters glance back
and the mast is in your hands. Who will arrive? Who will it be? The
captive spoils of dew and their moaning, the plunder of plant, that's
you. Do I cry: A horizon? No. Your bellowing morning sounds the
horn and the mountain gallops.

Who will arrive, O Earth, who will arrive?
An echo returns like a drunkard. An echo like a doll in a window
calls out to the passer-by. The soul burns its costumes. O house,
follow me so we can look out your windows into the flower vase.
O windowpanes, mask yourselves with me like a grin combing its
hair. No. A fool like me has passed through this dusk. A fool like me
has passed and comedy released its geese. This is deep. Deep. A
scream that crashes, like a cicada, into the tree of songs and the
conspiracy surrenders to its reflection.

Who will arrive?
Who will it be,
O Earth?
My spectre illuminates the lantern of spectres.
And resurrection scatters berries on the golden shroud.

8.

The lake, behind the door, knocking,
The desolation, behind my shield, smooth as a prince's robe, knocking,
Behind the waters are drummers and dolls made of fools' cries.

Mother, lay your baskets here.
Lay place like two slippers before the void for your drunken guest.
Father, let your vigil be long. Lay your head, like before, on the deep
wells where space is a bucket and dust a cloying rope.
Knocking on every door,
Knocking on this, the greatest ruin, and the flood decorated shields.

Revenge

a.

The coats are all there,

the winds all there,

footprints deep in the snow, and the snow all there,

the lamps, houses, last apparitions, all there.

So gather in your tame hands all they can hold of perfection

and strive so the scene may be a tamed echo.

b.

An unease, like morning, preoccupies those approaching my end,

and I—struggling under a great net—hang place—like a prisoner's

pants—on the line, that delicate line, running from the origin of

comedy to your moan.

c.

The abundance of naught is I and will is my suspicion.

d.

Rage is the sign of night and water a thought ahead of its own

completion.

e.

Like a shoe polished,

like a nickel doorknob,

thus is your scream.

Vocabulary

Day: anger masked in air

Wind: the steps of a word towards its secret

Sound: the ruin of form

Longing: gold scattered on the velvet of the end

Space: the shaper of light

Nothing: the humour of shadows languishing in its seat

Writing: violence testing the forgotten

Number: the yield of futility

Fruit: the tree's proof of a past that eludes all proofs

Mask: the manifest's moaning

Distance: repeated panting

Certainty: a murmuring on the other side

Resurrection: a childhood justifying reason

Gold: a bar fight

Life: a golden bullet

As for you, dweller in endings, don't stray too long, lest dinner get cold.

The Recklessness of Sapphire

(1996)

Ledgers of Plunder

(Excerpt)

With marble hands, the unknown strokes its desire.

Place grinds place,

so truth may attain, with conquest, its inheritance, O Death.

You! A Destiny with jagged edges, as if eternity had bitten into you
and bloodied time.

O you whose pain is a scale and whose annihilation is the blood of
oozing plums, probing audiences with the prudence of a comic root,
O Death.

You! Sharp as solitude.

O you, luminous inheritance of luminous oblivion. You shall follow
me, since certainty has led you, in your despair, to me and since
hope has incited me to apologize for the wound dealt you, O Death.

Every time we meet on the asphalt bend, Death, my neighbour,
you blow your little truck's horn at me in greeting? Every time I am
distracted from words, you send ink to investigate the eternal, like a
hired hand, there in the square where we argue with women who
share baskets of dandelion with angels?

Your silence is pure but you are a chattering partner, O Death,
and the paint is peeling from your festival chairs.

Don't leave this place; my eyes are on you.
Don't yawn, feigning morning sleepiness, for I am your insomnia
approaching eternity.
And lower your voice when you address Tomorrow, for our neigh-
bours are anxious, the gardens are anxious, and the deranged day's
hands begin to shake, serving crystal goblets to the mad.

You have asked me before, Death, to show you the coats countless
fathers have left behind in the closet.

[...]

When you clamour deliberately, I do not plug my ears. Instead, I
drum my fingers on the wood of the table, whispering to myself:
there it is, anxiety drawing attention to its apprehension of the
listless and their days.

When you clamour deliberately in the corridor of golden pillars,
slamming the windows and doors, pulling down the curtains,
knocking over the books stacked on desire's shelf, I do not plug my
ears. Instead, I show you cushions suited for play and copper chan-
deliers that jingle if plucked; I show you the framed mirror in which
you will be torn apart in order to be as you are now, seeking the
blow of horror that will grant you life.

[...]

Take your time, Death
From a height snow sprinkles its fires onto the mirrors
and day takes risks with the seal-breaking night.

Place is a ploy in your argument. It begs your palm for truth, joke by
joke. Winds catch your marble balls with bound hands . . .

Your caterpillar is of eloquence. Your air hunchback. And the
barbers around you clip twilight with scissors of water, grooming
the gardens like beards, O Death. They gently chide obscure desires
tied to their chairs where they growl like dogs.

Is this why you are unsure, O Death?
Is this why you despair like a garden that raises lures of rose and
crosses off numbers in air's ledgers.

[. . .]

Your hours are butterflies fleeing from time into colour.
And these schemes of yours? Cover them up, these schemes, these
trees, this light pouring out like the guts of a donkey. For you are
right—always proven right by the failures of our bodies—O Death.

You are right,
the gardens are right,
and the cell, the one that reads unto you the sermon of truth, is
right. So excuse me if I go and leave you behind like a grandfather
in sand, alone, ground by the indefinite cycle of your diminishing
existence, if I leave you with ghosts nudging you with their elbows,
as they pass through your lime corridors towards their arenas,
carrying shields you can't see—O Death.

But for now, remain my neighbour. Blow the horn of your little
truck hello every time you pass on the road to your errands. Let
abandoned certainty find company in you, the certainty that holds
up fences of neglected gardens with molten tin. Let loneliness itself
find company in you, loneliness that repairs with plaster the statues
piled up here, in the narrow distance between our house and
yours—O Death.

Stay, my neighbour, let us exchange spices made of crushed shark
bone. Let us share water from one channel,
    share one newspaper,
    one pack of cigarettes,
    the sullen ink,

and the hope forever chastened by dimpled Time,
like a child who has just broken the pencil sharpener with his teeth.

[. . .]

Everything in haste:

        Place

            Fortunes

                And eternity

All in a hurry.
And you are God's revealer, O Death.
Hastily, you survey the plundered and squabble with the decreed.

You've been killed.
I say, you've been murdered—O Death.

I can almost hear your fate crumble like marrow and melt like fat. You
are a father's clavicle cracking in fear of fatherhood and its righteous
roar.

[. . .]

I will leave you in the charge of death, O Death, in the scene gripped by the horizon, your silent bleeding, there where place is skinned by the ordinary. I will leave you in the charge of city hall and the wolf who stands erect before it, erect in his concrete, and by his sides rise the exchanges of blood in his Greek slumber, here, on the beach, astray by the corridors of the sea.

Do you hear the metal cranes?
Do you hear the mighty inspired by crisis to set the ledgers straight?

Don't you worry,
        All are gifts
                and eternity mints its own coins—O Death.

Digression in an Abridged Context

1.

Here the proofs, the fever.
With ink, you shade them from smug certainty.
You trap words, so proofs may sleep upon their quarrels.

No roosters here
but flame prancing like cockscomb
and rebel life warding off the hidden context of spirits.

No affliction here but rose;
no stray spear but universe;
lightning the night's disdain of place; and water mockery.
So why submit to higher wills, your ray broken,
why bestow upon pain the faith of the evening?

2.

Welcome, you bound wager!
Here, nothing, bleeding, smiles at its grandchildren.

3.

Your hope is his,
both drowsy in the praiseworthy warmth.
Both spent, pumpkin binds you;
as if your metaphors are the vanity of light in full fornication.

4.

Paths are pears on morning trees.
If the place jogs, jog with it:
Ahead of you are eternity's bicycles
and on your shoulders its empty sacks.

5.

So that opulence may gasp; so that nothingness be more pure:
You betray the light
listening to the protestations of joy on its way.

6.

Give her kisses.
Wretched, they find no way to her burning.
Give to her time that, shivering, assures you it's the tortured one.

7.

No denial,
life is your concealed number.

8.

Horizon this;
horizon that;
where they join, they are the crotch of the wind.

9.

Together:
You, snatched from your other others,
the ancient, ripe in its ancient vinegar.

10.

The cuppers are back.
The geese angry, the wind staggering, stuffy and choked.
Dwell not in this elegant panic as you roll space, testicle by testicle,
over the bridge and toss timeless seals through fissures in the
firmament.

Don't be stubborn as a schism.
Don't allow the schism in your hands to grow jerboa's fluff:

Here are swords, washed with the sperm of the dead,
And skulls, like air, hatch under the apothecaries' breath.
Here are tongues,

      orifices,

      kidneys,

      livers,

      and kneecaps,

in a course of light like mule hooves,
nations, fooled, scatter over dense genital wilderness.

And a single train,
descends from Lake Wan towards Alexandretta
bearing in its eighth carriage the heart of Shamdeen,
smiling upon the Kojars,
rolling over lands of Bhutan and the drowned seas.

Directions drop here, like crates of beet.

And rage—your laughing youth, who steadily, gracefully ravages
with tea cups the ancestors' markets and drives the shops, like goats,
to the abattoirs of light.

11.

In the direction of Muzan, dusk is your loaf of bread
and clouds your drums.

12.

Place is the gunshot of imagination that does you in,
may you recover; recover freely where loss is aspiration
where the universe drapes rags over certainty's threshers;
there, where wars, soft as squirrel fur, wave in gusts
of merciful controversy,
and nothingness—that stronger wing—gives cover.

The Kurds are there
in the echo of the shot that kills you,
may you recover.

Confrontations, Pacts, Troughs, and Others . . .

(1997)

Plastics

(Excerpts)

SLAUGHTER

The ancient brimming in jugs
and the eternal shaved like a crotch:
These two drag embers into the crevices and stitch the tempest
to the tempestuous.
Do the fates belch? There, meanings bang on the empty page with
their spoons and kick the words under the table with their bare feet.

There, the ancient shaved like a crotch
and the eternal brimming in jugs,

SHE

The earth, the bitch, shaking the wetness of ruins from her fur. The
earth, the bitch, arched in her marble sluggishness. No salvation.
The earth, the bitch with the green snarl, with veins dangling like a
tongue. Always herself. No salvation. She is fathomed in the most
resounding roar, crushed into barley and lentil. The earth—the
truffle, the frothing embrace, tight like a stallion's glans, like a
basilic vein, a frenzied exertion in the arc of dreamy old age. She is
she. The earth—the gasp, when the testicles knock at the clenched
opening. The earth, rebounding, blow after blow, over the eternal
rifts. The earth, sharpener of the second pang, curiosity with
chewed up edges. The earth—the sermon, the dull creaking of the
bloody sled.

Is she herself?
Return her to the bloodthirsty immortal.

IMPASSE

There they are:

The dead, the homes. The dead, balconies and alleyways, twisted
like tin bars. The dead, udders filled with the milk of chaos, the ones
carried on shadows of the burning, dusk after dusk, guides whose
bones have been branded by split seal. They, the dead, are bridges
lifted by ropes of regret to the levers of form. They read like fortunes
and signals. Caught in a blooming net, eavesdropping on the grand
ambush. They, the ones garnered in flame under the same eternal
arc, soft supple arc of a monument's breast. The dead, the amethyst
hooks, the golden buttons on ripped cuffs, the runners from one
broken ray to another, from one lock to another, from one suffi-
ciency to another. The dead, ice gliding sea lions towards the
debauchery of ice.

O! The dead, they, the impasse of the end.

Ran's Farm

OSTRICH

Like oblivion, towering, from the luxury of bird within,
over captive eternity.
In his shadow, the soil has two wings,
and certainty has little sisters wallowing in feather
or tossing the sublimity of presence around, like visions.
His obsessions are little ripples
and the etchings that captured the bulk of his form
liberated him into silk.

HEARTH WREN

Stretch over impetuous form
then drag these heavens
in a circle and break out pure as thought.
Return to the beginning of verse,
bolted onto your silver etchings,
in light, revealed and violated.

Gather these heavens.

PEACOCK

Terrify the unseen, terrify the forever of colour, undo the veins.
The place plunders ladders to slaughter
and the sky folds flap by flap.

SWALLOW

A tiger dragging the prey of eternity.

FLAMINGO

No sail binds his departure
No wind touches his mass, no guiding ray.

The day is his suitcase
and emptiness his things.

HOOPOE

A leisure that kept life warm. Is it
feathers that cover you?
Gather adversities like fluff
and sing the journey into a slow bleed.

A pattern, you are, summoned like a ghost
and bestowed a familiar form.

SAND GROUSE

The day will run on its dandelion leg,
leaping like a locust in your shadow,
cracked by the mirror of depiction.
The water wheels of plants will turn with the mules of air.
You are the shadow and the crutch of that air.

TURKEY

Muscle like labyrinth or deception,
and nerves like an insomnia of cloud.
Beware, you wildernesses of old! Don't fall asleep!

Don't ask me to master discipline, to master precision from now on.
The stupefied heights have torn their vests, and the stupefied
lowlands, like the stupid expanse, are useless, from now on.
My knees gave out, the sky gave out. The sky will be fixed by the
invaders, the defunct sky, the sky, that apron stained by the dribble
of blood. This sky, the chant of madness, the nightingale, the dance
of the nightingale on a dragon's tail. The sky, the jerking from one
belief to another. No proof of the sky, after this. No proof of a ladder
to it, no ladder to descend from it to the human, O Country.

Tearing and mending of the soul. The fury of stoning with ancestors'
bones, water ancestors, mud ancestors. The fury of stoning with
graves deceived of their corpses. The fury of the country, O Country.
You are the bags in which the disappointed gathers his clothes,
his tenacity, and the stolen throats of his children. Legitimacy
auctions you off, certainty is auctioned off within you. You are
the auction of shrines looted, graves looted, O Country:
a survey of property:

a castle in ruins
and invaders, invaders standing guard.

No clarification better than the citation of sand as an exhibit in
verdicts. Objections are easy now that we've started receiving
horror in rations. In rations we receive our lives, in iron ladles.
Upon inspection, only minor objections to the stubbornness of ruin.

Facile and negligible are the objections to divvying you up like cinder.
Call it murder, call it murder by the names of all your days from now on,
O Country . . .

[. . .]

Death is too restricting from now on.

[. . .]

No vigour will return me to what I was.

Not the mountain's loyalty,
Not the mountainous,
Not my grandfather, the mountain,
Not my grandmother, the forest,
      Not my brothers, the narrow roads,
          Not my sisters, the rocks burnished in the river stream.

          No dawn can return me to what I was.
No defeat, no victory,
No path can return me to what I was.

Not the good fathers
Not the good lovers,
Not the good murderers,
Not the good dead, whom death continues to announce to us as
prophets in the kingdoms of the dead. Not even they can return me to
what I was.

[. . .]

No one
will return me
to what
I was.

Chaos upon chaos: come back, O Country, to what astonishes and
dumbfounds, to what is only grasped in collapse.

Come back. I empty the splinters of numbers from zero's pockets.
The enemies are cruel like myths, O Country. I do not want a sky any
more. I do not want a land beneath me any more. Get my heart to its
feet. Get the unconscious roads to their feet. Stop this migration
from time to what time cannot know. End the feud of soil with soil,
the quarrels of gardens
and the shower of minutes shattered
by their own gavels,
O Country.

In shoes
or barefoot, slaughter completes its passage from the valley to the
mountain. No. Don't get my heart to its feet, O Country. Don't
allow it the chance of a last look at what will not return. It's likely
that I won't recognize the weight, after this. I won't recognize the
lightness, after this. Hands are air and hearts are air. Creation, a
migration of blasphemy to the justice of blasphemy. No sea here.
                                No sea there.
                                No valley here.
                                No valley there.

No mountain here.

No mountain there:

A country that closes the book on its long lines.

And the murdered won't rise to a task, after this. This is the harvest of labyrinths and the furnishings of the wind when it settles. Cheap moons in the markets. The murdered and their goods displayed on the twilight benches. The manners of the dead and the legislations of the dead in organizing death, like states. The graves, the exchanges, the amazement of the eggplant at the white teeth in the fearful's mouth, O Country.

The isolation of the universe, finally, O Country.

Many stables for the stone steeds. Many hives for the stone bees. Faith in the tortured stone, O Country. If asked to, I won't hand over the sky to anyone since I handed it over yesterday, with the hands of my certainty, to the beggars. Charitable death and charitable dead. This is water ashamed of itself, O Country. The sea weeping and the clouds wailing. You have been rewarded: Anger is the gods' rewards for tasks of death. And you have been relieved, for there is no fixing the cracks in the sky and its locks. Come here. There is no heart in your hand and no kisses in your pocket. So, rest when there is no heart in your hand, no kisses in your pocket.
When

no

door,

no

window,

no,

house,

no gardens,

no place;

when disgrace does not know you as it should

and hatred does not know you as it should,

and you don't know it as you should;

when evil is nothing but praise

and seduction is injury;

when bodies are folded like flags after the festival

and only hallucination can safely find an open road;

when the despicable day is necessary to receive the advice of the

despicable light,

and the experiments are all astrological

and nature is hexahedral in its suspicion like the purity in anger's

religion;

when there is no victor but the howling,

the depraved places and the depraved directions,

when the ending takes the course of the night

[. . .]

when the door is wounded

        and the halls are wounded,

                and the roads are a voice whose stories remain unfinished,

when mercy is impetuous with a temper like scales,
and the choir singers stand in rank on the blades of religion
chanting the farce,
when morals are for running with their feet, for reaching the edge
with their feet, for jumping with their feet

                                              from
                                              the heresy
                                              of a son
                                              to the
                                              heresy
                                              of a father

when the lapis lazuli beast lies in the nations of ruin,
        when directions are averse to direction,
                and cities to cities
                        and coasts to coasts;
When waters emulate birds, and what takes the same course as that,
        and what takes the course of the night,
                and the course of the unkempt thunderbolt,
                        and the course of praise committing suicide with its praised;
When the jokes, the farces there in the east, the fever,
        and the myth of kisses
                and the myth of man dreaming
                        and the myth of honey—come close, O Country:
nothing fits anything;
no hand fits another from now on.

[...]

You boiled. Vapour cooked the rice of meaning
and the directions became loose, only grasped in escape.
The morning has been demolished,
noontime shaken
and evening worn out. You boiled and cooked us like rice in all the
pots, O Country, arranged and organized. The appendices to wills
have been versified in gratitude to the inheritors. And the invaders,
       the invaders
       are the ones who hand the inheritance over. A sticky
       adhesive, you are. One that's been washed and lost its
       stickiness. You've been washed, O Country, O slender-
       boned Country. You have been washed into a resonance
       of thunder in the bones. No
                        rival
                        but oppression.
                        No
                        rival but necessity.

[. . .]

Never will I be asked for control mastered like precision mastered
from now on.
No! My grandmother the forest won't return me to what I was
from now on.

My grandfather the mountain won't return me to what I was
from now on.
My brothers, the narrow roads, won't return me to what I was
from now on.
My sisters the heavy rocks in rivers won't return me to what I was
from now on.

What an inheritance of bewilderment's blessings you are
O Country. My Country
You
O Country.

All the Doors

(2017)

Divide the doors among you by hand-lengths.
Distribute them to your offspring in equal heights.
Painted or bare,
the squeaking of their hinges is destiny scratching on tin.

Door, painful when open
Painful when closed;
Painful are the doors. Ugh:
They are homes weeping over your hearts in ruin.
The fading outline laments you; you who stand in a line like doors
That slap those entering and slap those exiting. O you narrators of
stuttered truths, you narrators of stuttering, wearing your wounds
and your dignity as medals of honour side by side on your chests.

Chastise the water chastised by death.
Scold the hidden or provoke it. No slacking:
Proud you are of this burning that recalls old fires in the semiotics of ash;
proud you are of the thunder that ripped wings; of the sand that
narrates with its channels histories panting with thirst.
Proud you are of the evasions of water
and the evasions of blood as well,
proud of the labyrinth—the price of your decrees, the legislator of wolf laws.

You are proud of luxury, the trigger that rips through you when pulled,
Proud of the legacy of reptiles,
the lineage of hyenas,
the pacts of raptors,
the covenants of ants
and the honour of pebbles in the wild.

[. . .]

All are doors,

doors that do not upright the shadows flung against them by trees

in the square.

Convex doors,

concave doors,

low, seasons must enter them hunched,

high, lands climb to them on ropes of war.

Doors, only to be broken by kicking feet

or bashing skulls.

Doors levelled into earth, opened unto the press of darkness

and water wheels.

Doors with the cunning to shut by padlock of fever

or the cunning to open at the sound of a grieving voice.

Doors tightly shut like the months of war,

Doors, fallacies of categorization,

proofs in the sandalwood of the enchanted forest.

Doors that will not be shut before the kings finish slaughtering

their banquet guests.

What is not a door is a door by the trick of a door in camouflage.

What is not camouflage is a door.

What cannot be grasped is a door. Ugh:

Bring forth the platters and the jugs, you who have been promised keys,

like despair, for closed doors.

You, the ones dreaming of a door,

the ones stabbed in your sides by promises.

Arrange seats in the eternal orchard with the cob fence.

Close the doors,

Fold what you do not know into what you know.

Exchange doors—you are the measure

excluded

from

the

vigilance

of keys.

[. . .]

Lean into the doors with shoulders made of northern stone. Ugh:

No door without grief.

No door without a threshold that grief has already crossed or will soon.

Lean on its creaking.

A door without creaking is a door emptied of grief

or flooded with grief until gagged.

The door

feels no

disgrace.

Disgrace is behind the door

or before it.

[. . .]

Bring ash, if it collapses, to its feet.

Bring defeats, if they collapse, to their feet.

Bring anxiety, if it collapses, to its feet.

Bring catastrophe, if it collapses, to its feet.

Bring disaster, if it collapses, to its feet.

Bring injuries, if they falter and collapse, to their feet.

Bring battles, if they collapse, to their feet.

Bring hell, if it collapses, to its feet.

Bring

the gods

if they

collapse

to the

feet

of their

slave boys.

[. . .]

Whitewash on everything,
or the splatter of whitewash.
A pouring of paint on everything.
A stroke of paint on the brooms of catastrophe
and a drop of paint on the dragon's tail.
O you, pure ones, lustful in your purity,
you who are crushed by purity,
you who smoke purity,
you,
slaves
in the slave
light.

Fruit has no resolve
nor does the open road.
O you broken ones,
like the glance
one wretch casts
at another.

[...]

The weather is right for sleeping under bridges.
The weather is fickle like bridges
mystified like bridges.
Friday collapses on top of Saturday,
and Saturday on top of Sunday,
and the other four support each other so as not to collapse.
O mountain people, your voices are the frolicking of grass in the wind.

They all trace their fathers with the wrong lines,
since they have only known them as mistakes unavoidable in drawings.
You, violent in the shade, peace-loving
when you
walk
in the company
of elephants.

[. . .]

Only be what the doors were,
what the doors are
and what the doors will be.
Only be the locks in survival.

[. . .]

Rags that are cities,

and villages that are unwearable tatters.

Fates are roads you travel in the traffic of wretched fortunes.

As for the beer froth, it's been the same froth since beer found its faith.

Ugh:

Remedy the burdened air with air

and colour with colour

and ruin with ruin

and disaster with disaster

and lack with lack

and wreck with wrack

and punctured ships with the confounded sea

and a scream with a scream.

Remedy

the universe

with an excess

of its improvised order.

[...]

All are doors,
door to the slaughterhouse: the accomplished calm after the
slaughter storm,
the tranquillity of drowning in the languor of drowning,
the butchers' caution not to scratch the bones.

[...]

All are doors:

Doors to factories that furnish hell.

Doors to moon factories and god factories.

Doors to factories of paradise,

To factories of beds for paradise

Factories of six-way intercourse quivering until the beds

in paradise collapse. Woe unto you:

Bring the massacre back to its feet if it collapse.

Bring the battles back to their feet if they collapse.

Bring the defeats back to their feet if they collapse.

Bring the burning, if it collapse, back to its feet.

Bring

the gods

if they

collapse

to the

feet

of their

slave boys.

Lineages of Animal

(2019)

Dog

Ingratitude is blond.
Disobedience blond.
And you, who are you, subtle like hunger,
true like the outline of ruins under sand.

You are the loyalty of river reeds, but you've been
tricked into obeying the loser with the upper hand,
obeying the ingrate as well as the grateful.
Have you been humiliated into obedience? You are drawn
to the pastime of boredom with the bored, the pastime of loneliness
among the lonely,
of disappointment with the disappointed,
of failure with the failed,
of weakness with the weak one who controls you,
the pastime of compensation with he who only submits to compensate
for lack.

You are made to imitate your mimicking master. Grab the leash
from the hand that walks you, the hand that's proud you bring his
newspaper to his house between your teeth, proud you pick up the
dropped bones of his existence.

Peel your shadow from the shadow of the master and become poetry, poetry of baaaaarking or of piss.

Turtle

Time, at ease, slowly

Silk, inspirer of the principles of execution, slowly,

Echo, eternal kicking at the sides of the soul, slowly,

Cultivation of alphabet in rows of rossa and iceberg, slowly,

Gods, the quarter-gods in deception, slowly,

Annulment of meaning, slowly,

And more, an abrogation of lifetimes, an annulment of death, slowly.

What, what is in slowness, in abandon? The miracle of turtles.

Flea

Pressurized humpback lode of blood,
it sprints across the warm beds of tyrants,
weaver of precise restlessness, happy with its plenty, with its insomnia.

You are the conscience of blood,
its tailor,
the barber of its elegant red.
You are blood's satisfaction with being.
You
are
blood
alive
with the life within you
and the life within that.

Fish

Leave the fish alone.
Don't interrupt its fabrication of water wounds,
its fabrication of escapes for water from the isolation of water.
Don't interrupt its shaping of water into a record of migrations.

Let it prepare for its seasonal journey across the water dunes
with herds of deer in the grey blue of the sea's angry swell.

Each is busy with its seasonal guests:
the migration of rage,
of panic, with its sand-necked birds,
of hearts,
of gold,
of roads, ports, the migration of the sky
to the sky,
the sky,
the sky in mirrors.

The seasonal migration of sea,
of ruin,
the earth's second migration to oblivion.

Does the fish migrate like these
or in their wake?

Let the fish be, prepared for its journey, like the universe prepared for
its own, prepared to herd its cows to the graze lands of the dark.
Let it be, in the addiction of fins to words of love.

Salt dates hang on the palm trees of the sea:
Let the fish circle their fronds, and in the sea markets
exchanges of foam coins ring, coins etched by waves.
The purchases
of water for water,
air for air,
fatigue for the fatigue of coin,
madness for madness,
blue for blue,
defeat for defeat,
bleeding for bleeding,
mutiny for mutiny,
insult for insult in those markets of water, markets very much
like the forests of grass
where fish hide from the pursuit of eel.

Homo Erectus

So, you have an axe, then. You have a spear, up on two feet, a hunter with a heart that flutters like the wings of avian prey and falls like animal feet on damp grass and mud and rock. But your past still walks beside you on all fours.

You are the first wanderer among inventors of stone axe and spear. Out of the south, which split coincidently from the other empty vectors, directions into which you divided a migrating race, conceived from intercourse of air with sand.

So there, you have a mind with you—the mind of an axe.
And there, you have a mind with you—the mind of a spear.
And there, the first hunter is with you—the mind of the weary blow and ferocious ploy.

You have bequeathed to the descendants their desires in spoonfuls between their teeth. Hunters and peddlers of wounds, thieves who steal from death his door keys, his tobacco and the final pages of his account book.